Poetry for…

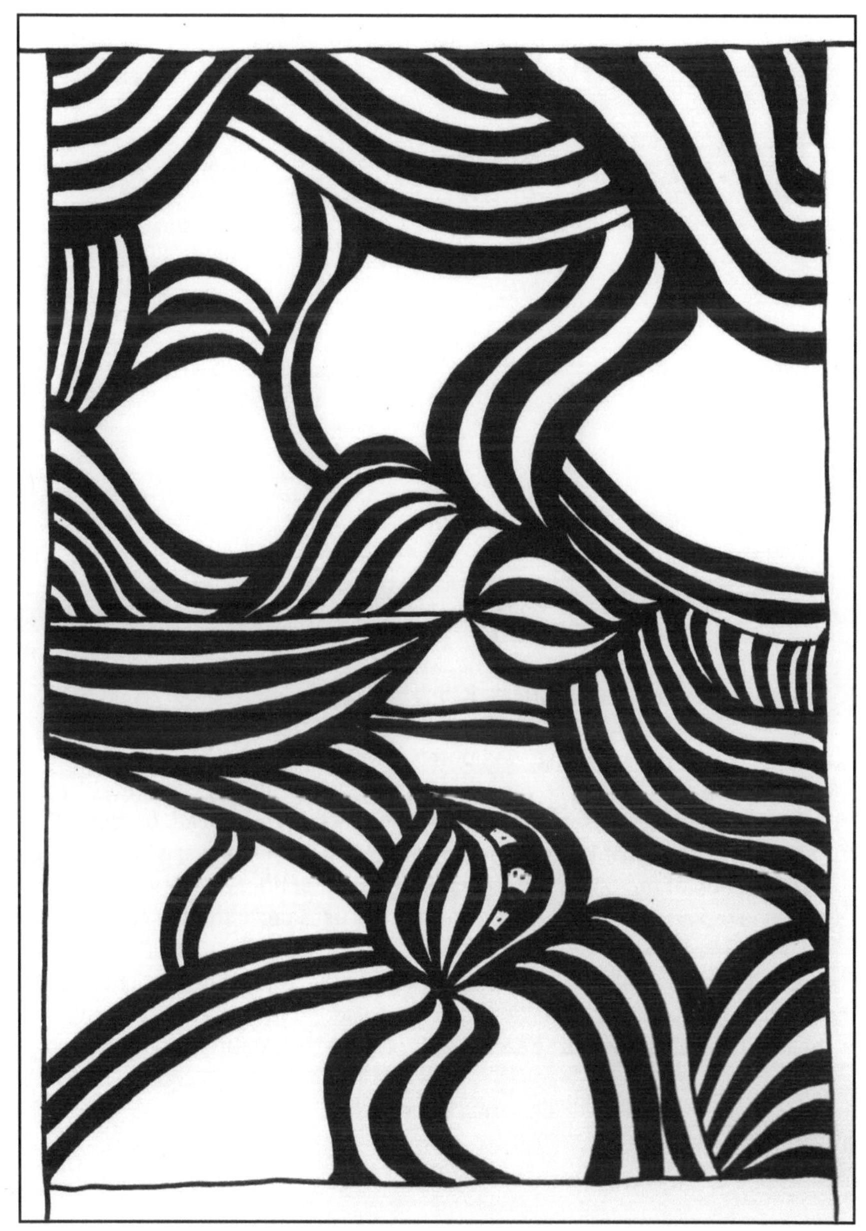

MICHEL BELLAICHE

Paperback: 978-1-963050-94-3
eBook: 978-1-963050-95-0
Library of Congress Control Number: 2024901266

Ordering Information:

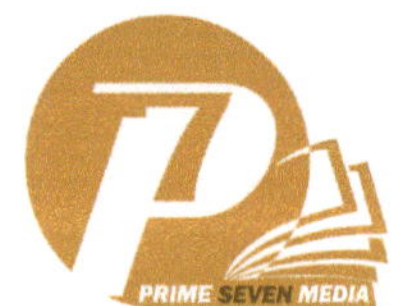

Prime Seven Media
518 Landmann St.
Tomah City, WI 54660

Printed in the United States of America

Table of Contents

Introduction

I was born many years ago In Tunisia. My family and I had to escape the country in the early sixties because of political upheaval. I was 10 years old, a refugee, and have never been back to Tunisia since. Some kind of trauma, maybe.

This early experience as a displaced person at a so early age have contributed strongly to what I became, rebel and perpetual expatriate.

I became a French citizen at 16, when France gave citizenship to my father as a recompense for his actions during WWII.

I have since seen many lands. I have met many people. I have been many times in love. Sometimes love lasted. Other times it passed away into indifference and forgetfulness. Other times again love lasted and gave great joy and hurt.

All this has made me what I am.
I am a wordsmith, always have been.
I am a painter of instants with words and sound.
My words are extracts from my days, distillation from my years, tears of time frozen in instants.

Years ago, in 2012, I met a very wonderful lady of Algerian origin. A beautiful story was very close to have happened. It did not. We remain good friends.

My friend is Kabyle. The Kabyle are the original inhabitants of Algeria long before the arrival of Romans or Arabs.

They call themselves and their language Amazigh. During one of our talks, she explained to me that my family name means "Son of Life" in Amazigh.

I found this very beautiful. It also surprised me but, being born in Tunis (Tunisia,) my father's family being an ancient Jewish Tunisian family, and Tunisia being close to the Algerian region of Kabylia, there was some sort of logic in that.

The Amazigh have always revendicated their difference in Algeria (although it is not always easy for them doing so).

The sign the Amazigh use to manifest their identity is the one that I attach here. It is a prehistoric sign found in caves and parietal art in their region.

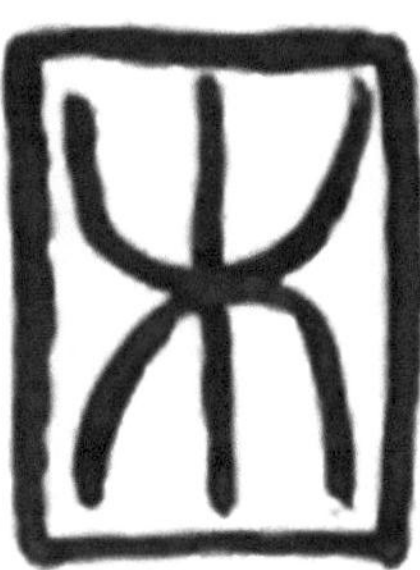

I have since adopted it as part of my signature on my paintings.

For a look at more paintings than those included here, visit www.bellaiche.net.

Dates

Below, for information for those interested, the date where each text was composed and each illustration created (when it is known).

Illustrations

Cover:	Brise-vague	2013
Page 4:	L'étonnante expérience d'un rêve	2013
Page 12:	Il y avait une ville	2020
Page 15:	Emperor on a yellow field	2021
Page 18:	Jours tranquilles	2015
Page 23:	We the damned – We the forgotten	2015
Page 32:	Portrait Ridicule	2023
Page 35:	Self-portrait with blues	1999

Texts

Page 7:	Power song	1995
Page 8:	Beggar	2001
Page 9:	Names	1998
Page 10:	I am dazzled	2001
Page 13:	Soul's complaint	unknown
Page 14:	Shadows	unknown
Page 16:	Love in black	unknown
Page 17:	Confusion	2002
Page 20:	Preach	1994
Page 21:	Song of I	2000
Page 24:	Future Samba	1999
Page 25:	Sweet Singing Corpse	2010
Page 26:	I'm on my way	2004
Page 27:	Rite and sorrow	2005
Page 28:	All that we have	2007
Page 30:	Return to war	2005
Page 31:	Danger time	unknown
Page 33:	Balkan Ballad	1997

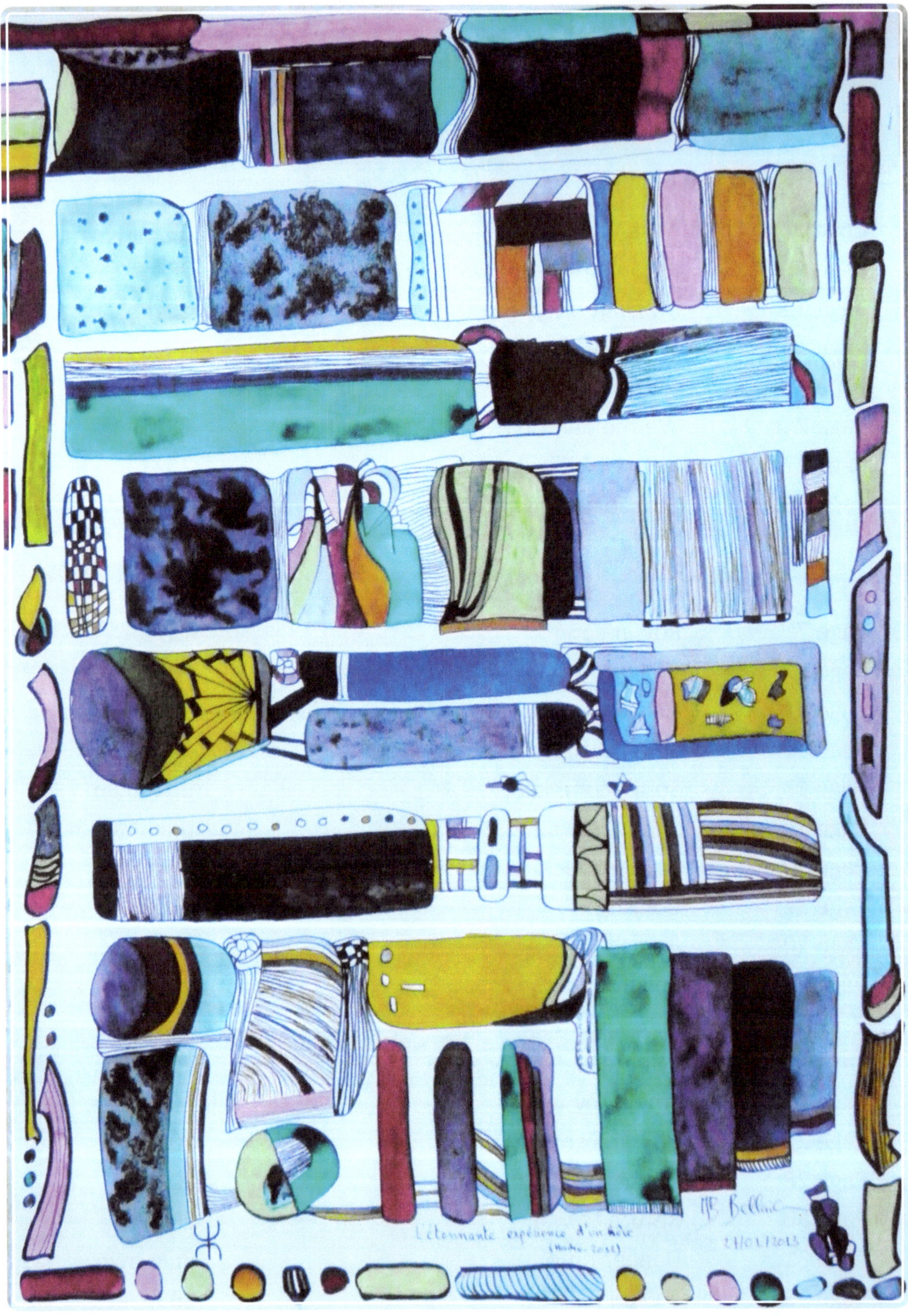

Talking

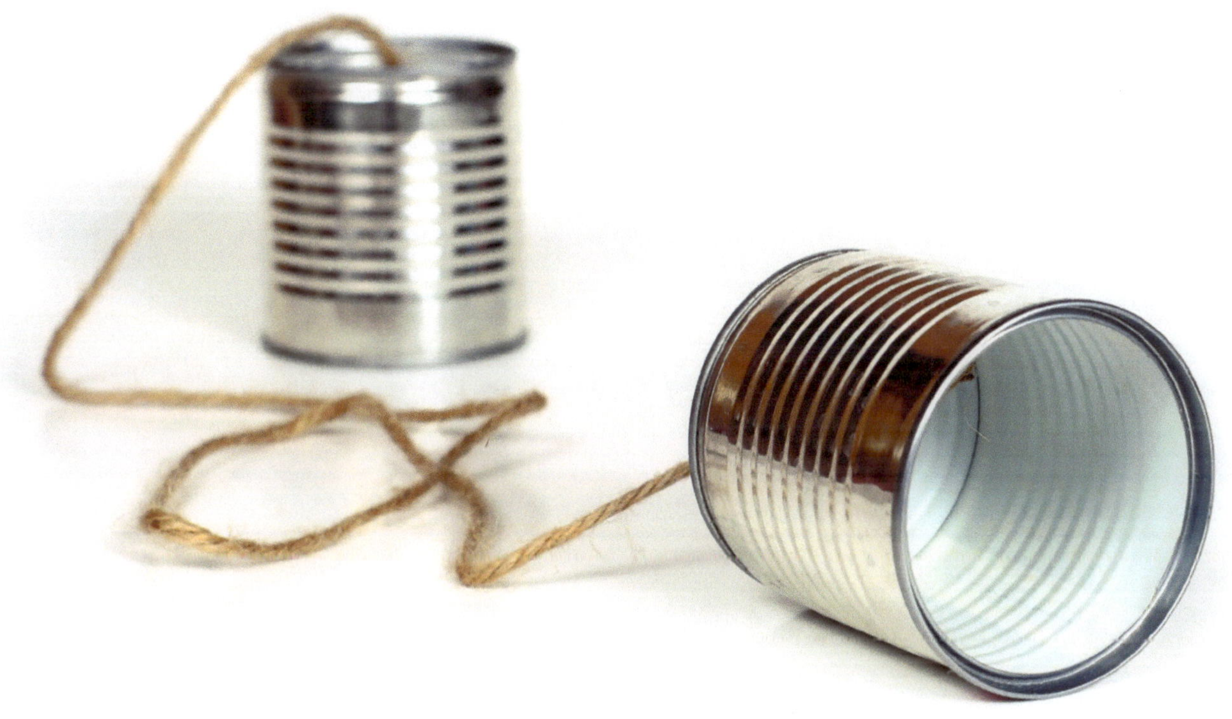

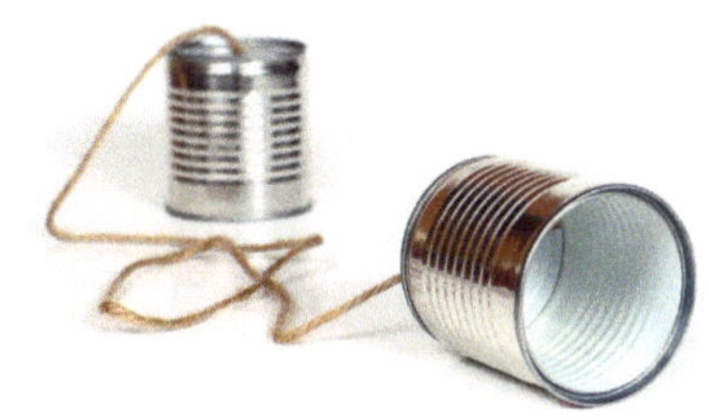

Power song

Song of praise,
Song of joy and freedom,
Song of force, song of heat,
Song of heart unlimited.

Song of power,
Song of willful learning.
Sad song of the days to pass,
Shanty.

Wondrous song of the years,
Days of earth.
Song of power vibrant and rising.

Cold song of the days to pass.

Song of praise, of joy, of freedom.

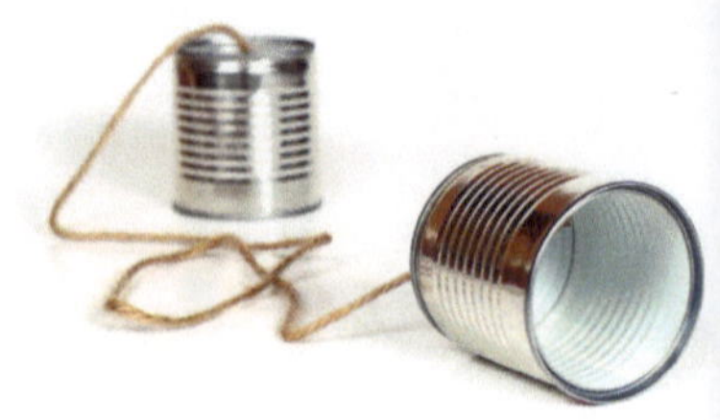

Beggar

I'll give you ten pounds for the story of your life,
I said to the guy in the woolen cap, begging loudly,
halfway down the stairs leading down and down
to the gents' lavatory out there at the train station.

I don't want to sell you my life he said,
and his face was gray, and his hands were trembling.

My life is all I have left he said,
reclining on the badly swept stairs, leading down and down
to the gents' lavatory back there at the train station.

My life is not worth a penny he said,
and his eyes were dull, and his odor was rank
and he pulled back his woolen cap down to his eyes,
and he said no more.

So, I left the guy in his woolen cap,
begging silently and with trembling hands,
and I walked back up the stairs that were leading down and down
to the gents' lavatory out there at the train station.

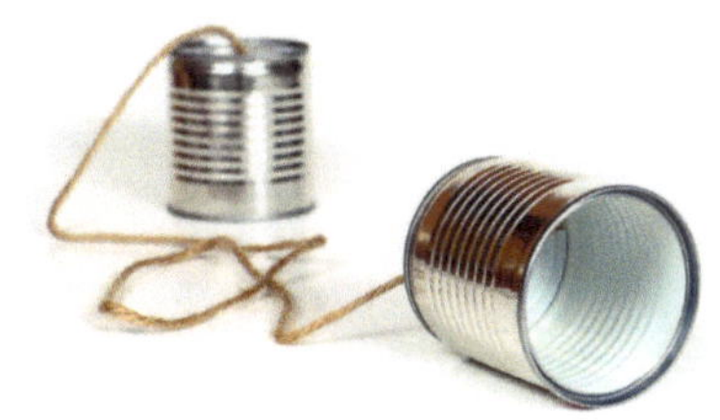

Names

My name is Fury.
I am permanence,
      I am song.

I am a fruit of remembrance,
I am the search and the question.

My name is Quest.
My name is Fright.
I am a spark throughout darkness.

I am the word and the retreat.
I am the prayer and the gloom.

My name is Cry.
My name is Hope.
My name is promise and surrender.

I am the sound of ideals,
And I offer profound comfort
In the depth
      In the depth
            of the richness of your soul.

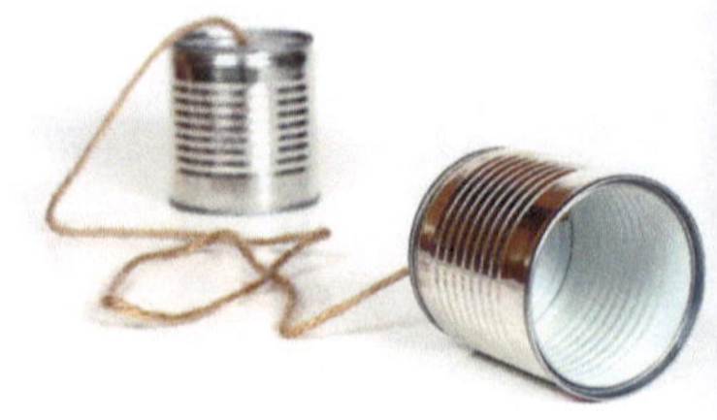

I am dazzled

I love cities, and the noise, and the crowds.
They make my pulse wither and my head spinning hard.
I love the bustle at all times, and the dust, and the cabs,
and all these shiny little lights, looking just as worlds
turned back on themselves.

I love the hustling, the hardship and the slums.
There are dock lands,
there are rivers brimming with slime
and refuse and dust gone bad.
Buses rusting, publicities in an odor of gasoline.

Loads of girls in summer dresses. Keep on running, not looking back.

There are those nights of ductile light, neon fresh, green and lime.

Peep shows, the light is on.
There are models on the first floor, it says on the hand-written sign.

I love cities of golden age, where misery is well hidden.

Boasting fumes of gasoline whenever lights are turning bright.

A crying girl; what have she seen? Where has she been?

I am feeding on the obese thoughts
cranked out on streets and boulevard.

The spiked hair of the Asian boy bragging loudly in his T-shirt.
That is violence, and pain, and rain.

.... I am dazzled (cont.)

Standing so quiet on a street corner,
the fat girl in a flowered dress, neither a look nor a word.

The fire truck lumbers, sirens ablaze, caught in traffic.
Where is the fire? Where is the urge?

I love cities of golden lights, dazzled, cabs rushing by.

A drunk lying near the corner, right under the theatre marquee.
Vomit lit by neon lights.
Nobody should have to die that way.

Il y avait une ville

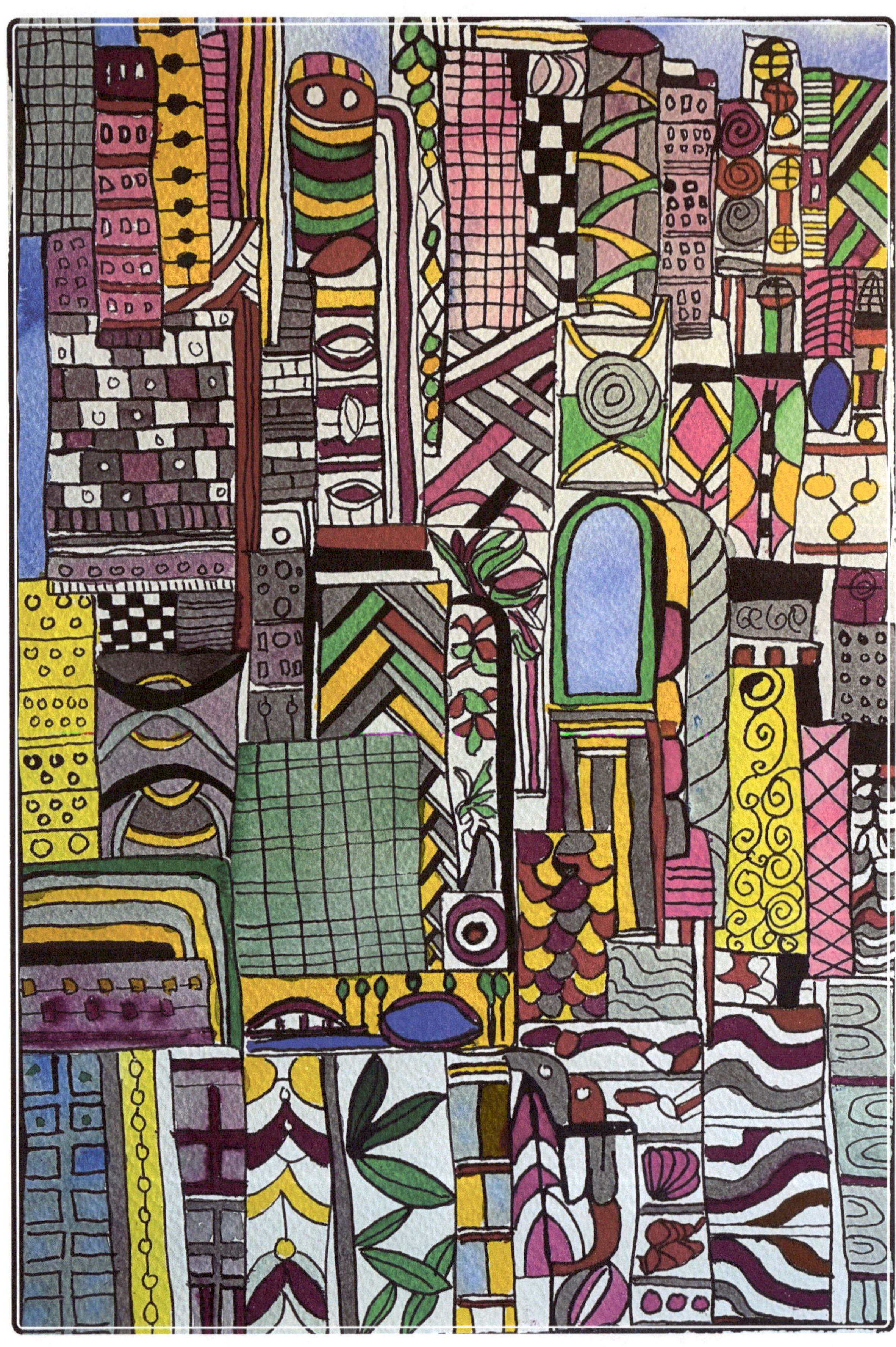

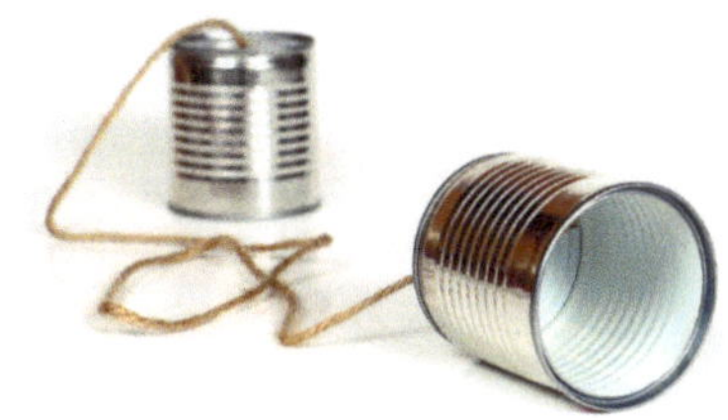

Soul's complaint

Rinse my soul.
Rest my everlasting, ever tiring soul
Rest the brushes of my heart.
Reward the broken pieces of the stones of my life.

Rest my soul and my eyes and my hands.

In the everlasting rage of the heart of my heart,
break my soul and my limbs and my mind.

Work back-to-back on the path to destruction.
Rest my souls of the toils,
of the tears,
of the years.

Rinse my soul everlasting,
Rest my heart ever wondering.

Wonders and marvels remake the broken pieces of yesterday's miracle.

Rinse my soul on the gates of heaven.

The colors of hell are taking their toll
of toils and labor,
of pain and wonder.

Clean my soul to the gates of heaven.

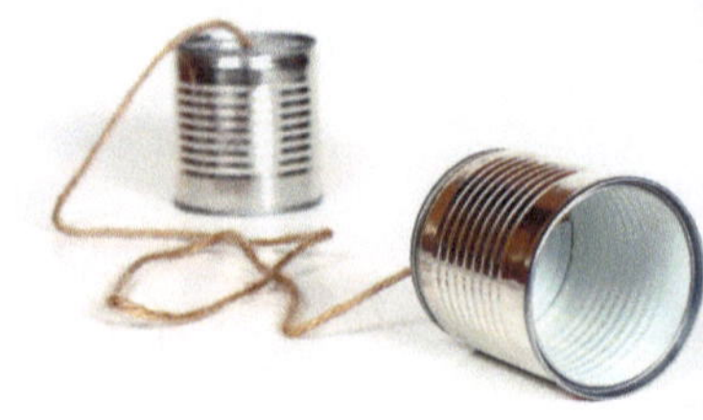

Shadows

I had heard that people
were islands untouched,
as passing in a street
at evening shadows.

Windows are glimpsed stars,
unharmed and distant.

You are looking at lives
through windows on those streets.

I have known of long nights
redolent and solemn.
I have heard of people
Cruising through these island streets.

Emperor on a yellow field

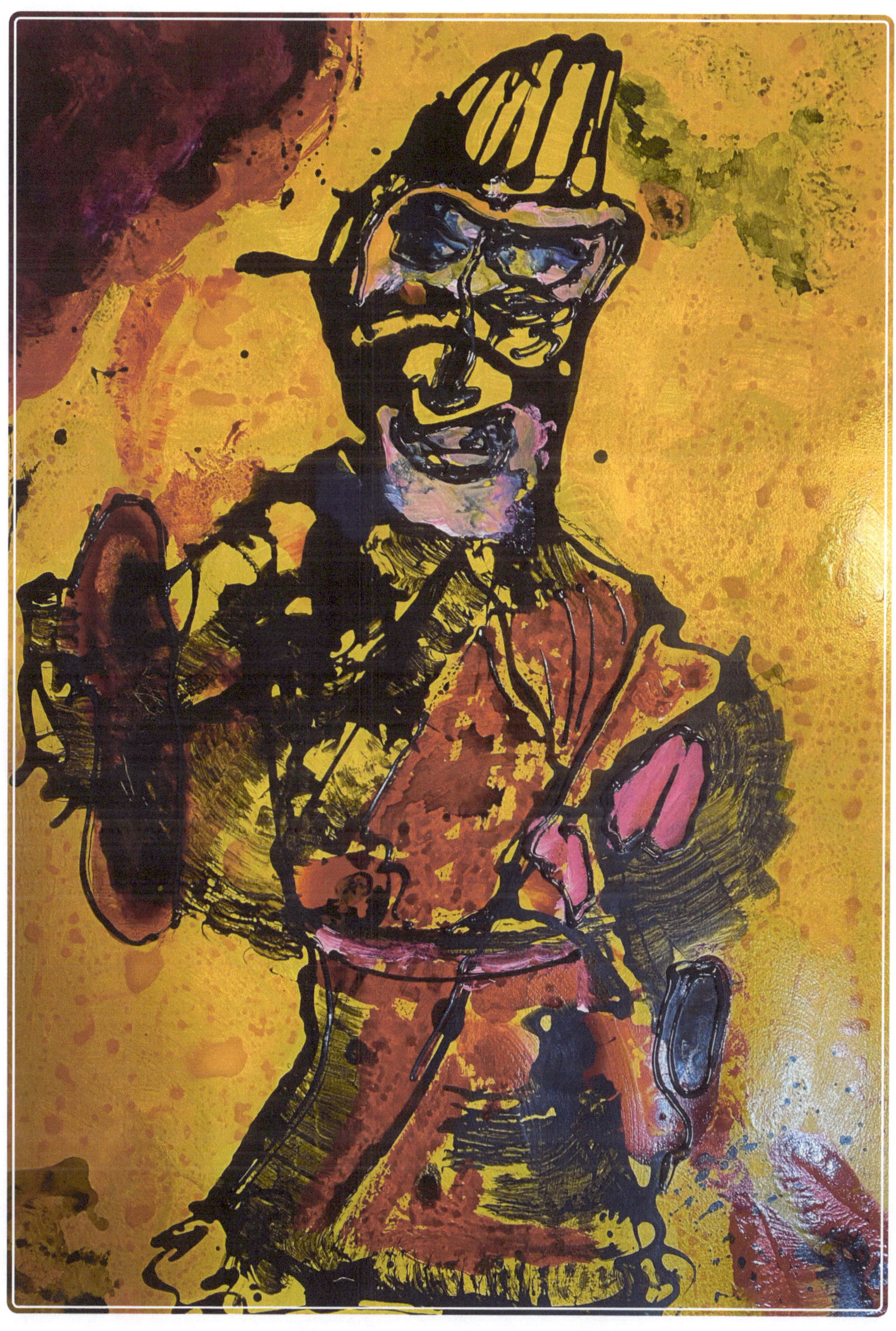

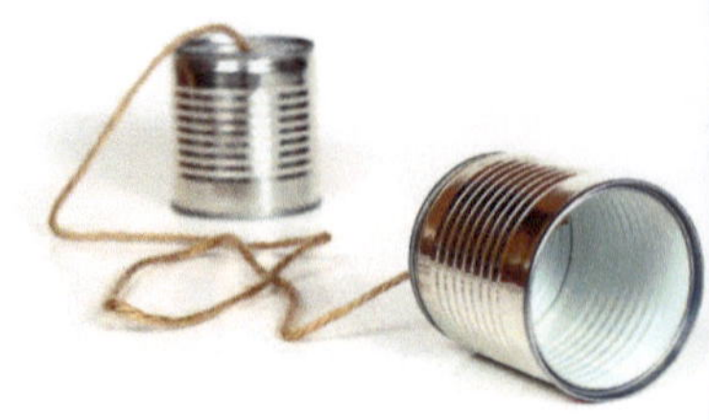

Love in black

Love is a drunken metaphor.
Old photographs in black and white,
where every scar is so visible.

Every secret is black and white,
Every hand remains hidden.

Return, jewel of forever.
Every love remains secret.

Old photographs in black and white,
where everyone returns your stare.

Remove that hand, wounded, perfect,
precious light in black and white.
Who knows desire?
Who wants remorse

Love is a song in black and white.

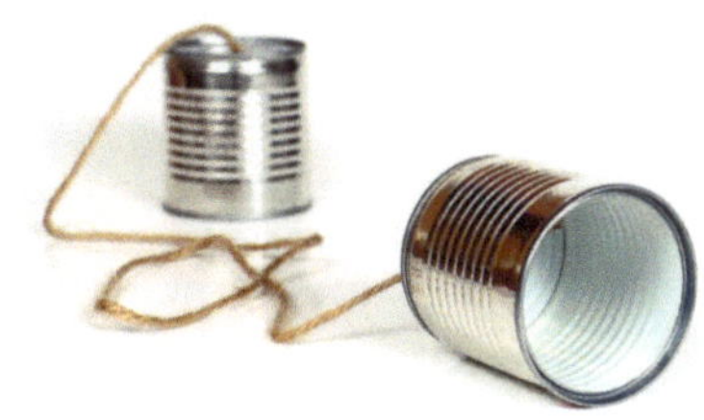

Confusion

It was a world of confusion; I was gripped by passion,
a master of spinning illusions, wondering about collusion.

What is evil and what is rage?
What is despair and where is loss?

Tell me of seagulls, of waves, of thunder.

I shall reply with rocks and with clouds and with fires.

What good is blue?
How red is fear?
How far can you teach the limit of gunfire?

Tell me of valleys, of rivers, of winds.

I'll pluck your burned soul off the coals of your life.

Jours tranquilles

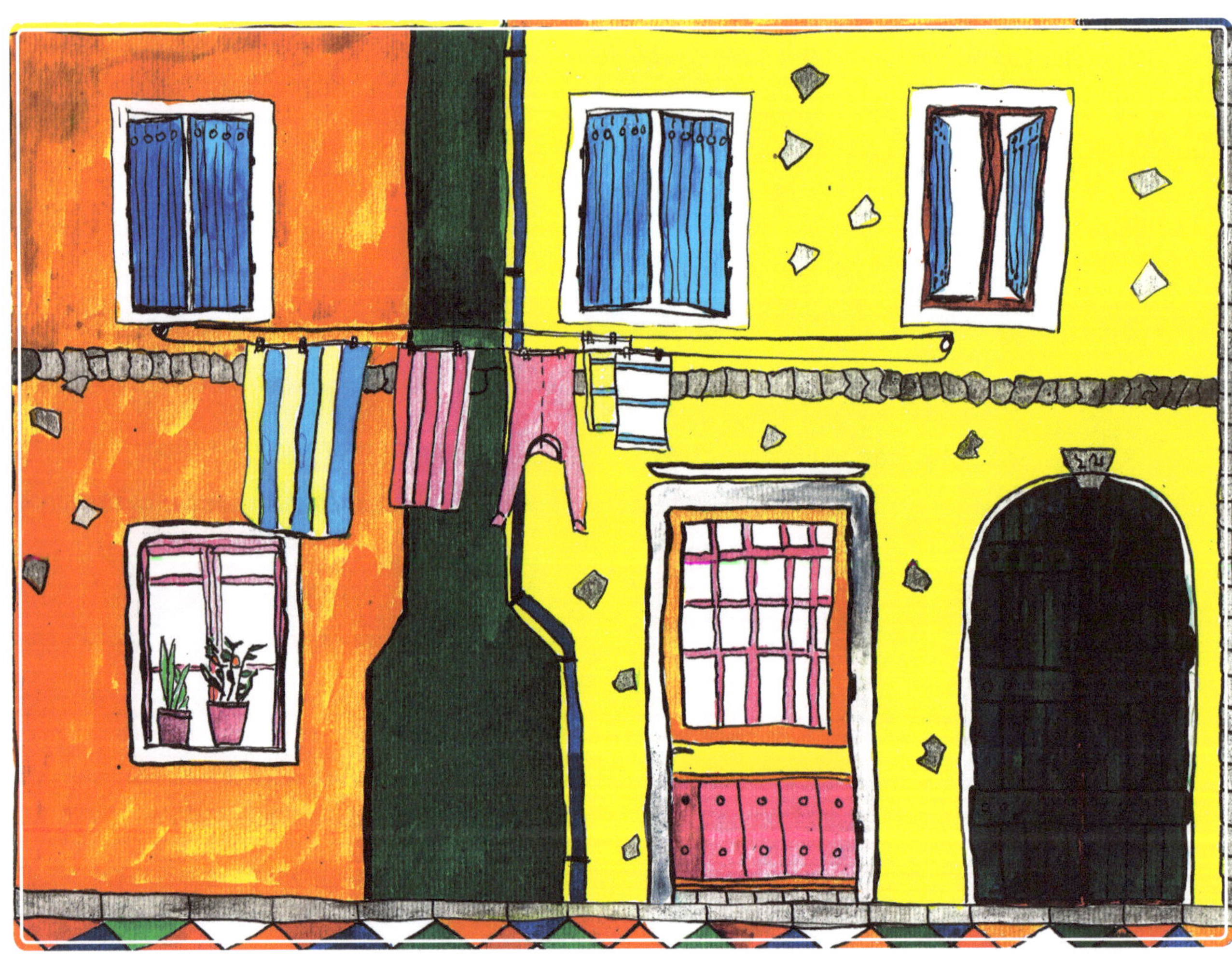

Be true

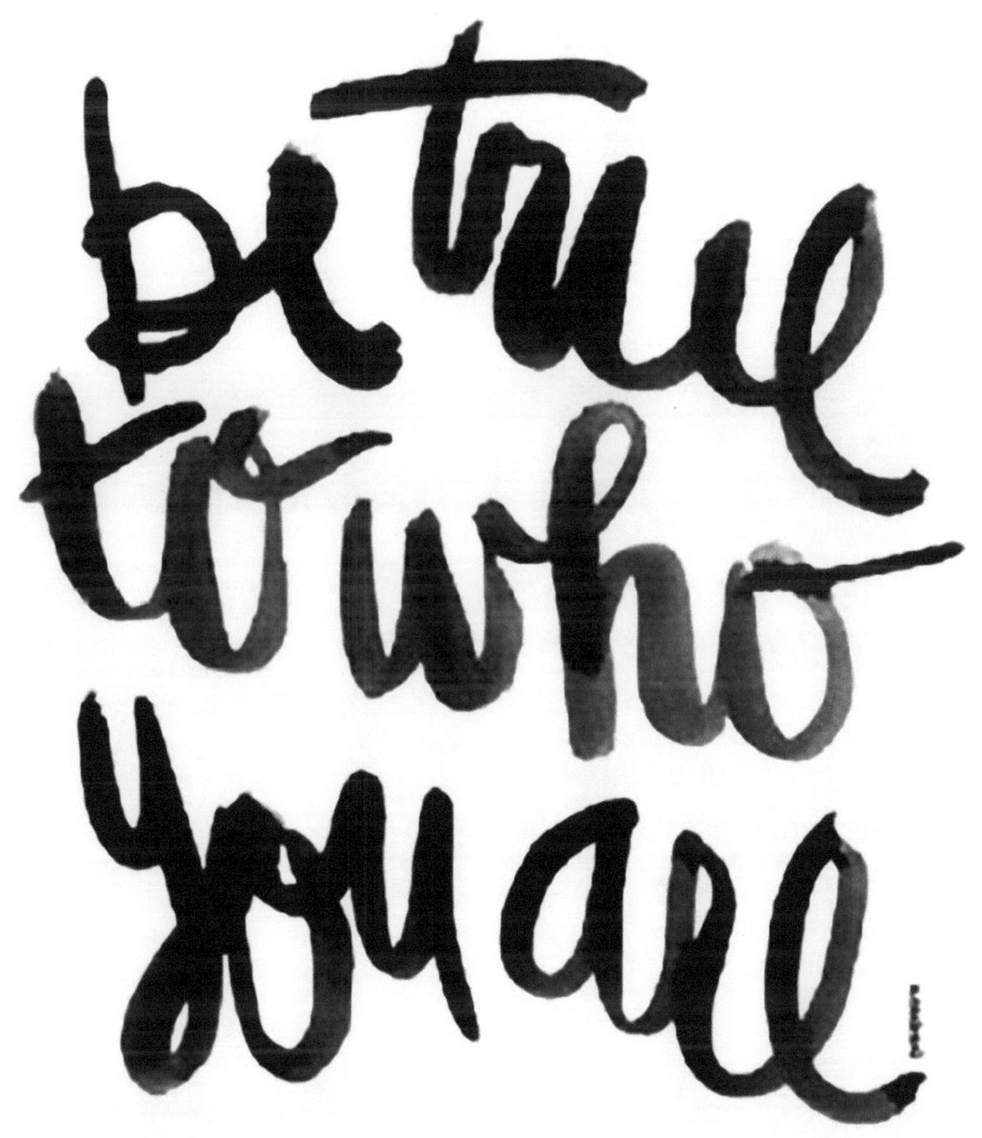

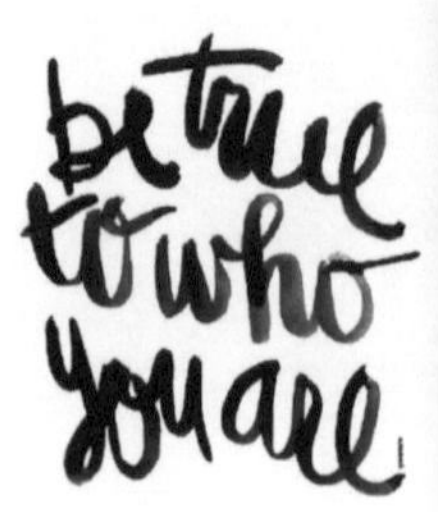

Preach

Talk to the rocks and talk to the mountain.
Cry preacher, cry!
Your time is not near yet.

If you walk to the sea and understand the waves,
If you caress the winds and burn forests,
Listen to me then.
I'll teach you the limits of blindness and greed.

If you have been wounded through the harsh words of love,
If you felt on your brain the searing light of truth,
If your despair is high,
If your trust is famished,
Listen to me then.
I'll guide you through madness, I'll guide you through blue.

Listen to me then.
I'll teach you the meaning of blindness and greed.

Cry preacher, cry!
And do not surrender.
There are those who believe,
There are those who deny.

Tears of lead and of gold tear your world asunder.

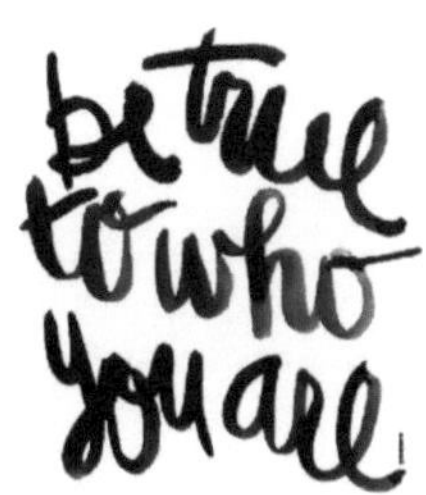

Song of I

In the arts were flowing the low imprints of glass.
Pure are the willing grasses,
Mythic as reverse fires in dew,
Irreversible,
Moving as in a glide.

Esthetic clouds of broken eroticism,
Sliding as a thigh adversely revealed.

I repeat!
I repeat.
I repeat.

More as a moving branch,
More as a frozen note.
More resounding again, icy and perfect.

Insects of perfect memory
Resounding in my mind.
Cruelty, brazen, audacious.

I repeat.
I demand.
I pray.

Turn reverse acrobatic of dance.
Ballet is black and mauve,
As excruciating colors.

.... Song of I (cont.)

I demand.
I repeat.
I scream.

I repeat.
I repeat.
I repeat.

This is exigency imperfectly woven.
This is what should have been, but brutally exposed.

Power is running low,
Theatrics as movement,
Recurrent, exigent,
Erotic and solemn.

I insist.
I demand.
I create.

This is powerful dough,
Just right for building dreams.

We the damned – We the forgotten

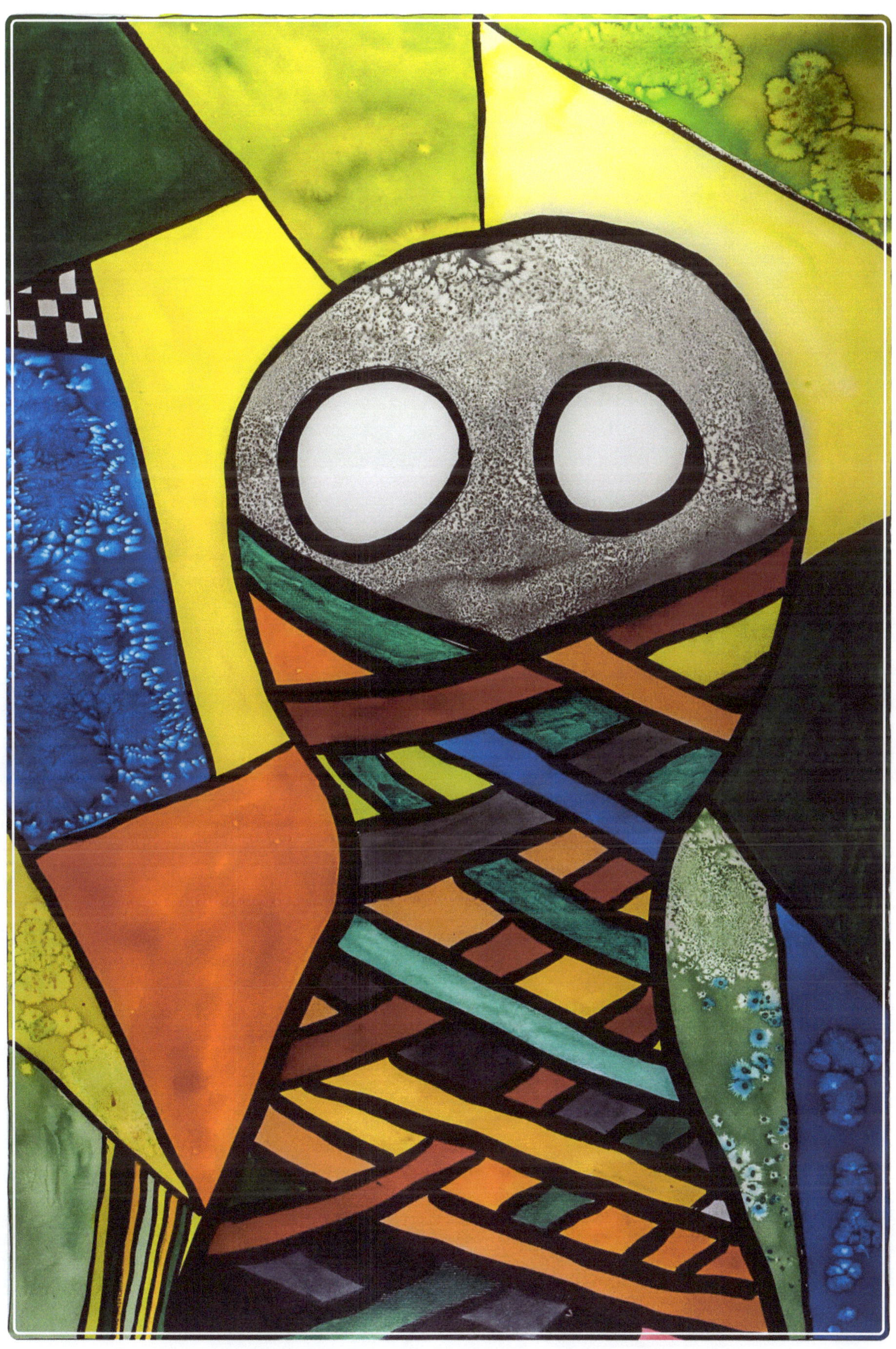

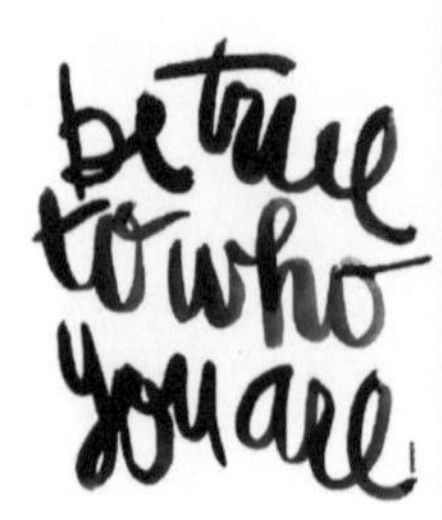

Future Samba

I won't get to my grave on the hollow wings of pride.

Come friends. gently gather,
    let us wonder just once again.

Let the enticing dark play its entwining song of Samba saxophone.

I won't rejoice nor will I cry.

Come friends from far corners,
    let us marvel yet one last time.

The pain is no burden.
These tears don't need blur the arriving vision.

Yet, wonders on the brink forever stay shrouded.

I shan't get to my grave while still looking backwards.

I shan't walk to my grave with a grin and a laugh.

I shan't rejoice nor shall I cry.

In this once again fluid darkness,
    None will recoil,
        None will move.

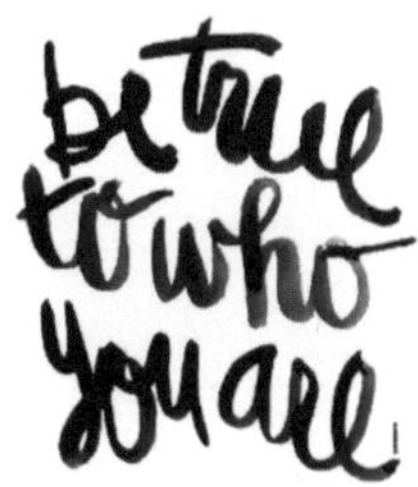

Sweet singing corpse

I am just dead.
I have just died,
right this minute,
as fresh a corpse as ever I saw.

There was a wind —not to wonder,
but now there are no more ventures.
The crushing wheel of boredom
has reentered our towns and lives.

There was a corpse by the river,
just where the flames had stopped last year.

Do I recall the fresh perfumes
just distilled from these bodies?

Am I to mind, as in a dream,
what has returned from the waters?

I am that corpse,
just freshly dead,
right this minute,
as in a dream.

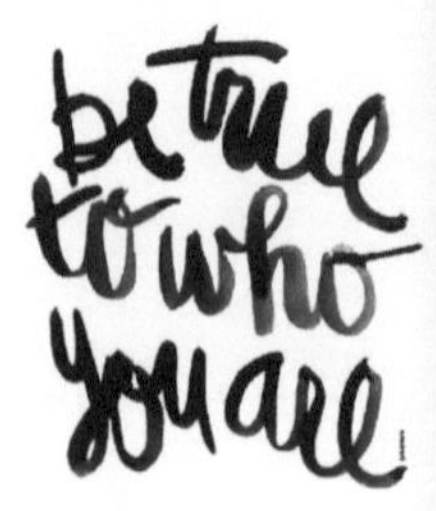

I'm on my way

I got myself some purchased love, my love.
And the night was all grayness.
I bought myself a tiny bit of love, my love.
There is but little joy in purchased love, my love,
Only restraint and foggy smiles.

I bought myself a line of dust, my love.
I bought myself a line of sun.
There is no joy in purchased sunshine, my love.
There is no sun beyond the dust.

I bought myself a three-course dinner, my love.
I bought myself some room service.
There is no joy in lone dinners, my love.
I bought my life at the breakfast lounge.

I bought myself a quick final, my love.
I purchased a rhyme and the Last Supper.
There is no lust in purchased death, my love.
There is no joy in looking back,
Only a road and a muddy pond.

I bought myself a crown of dust, my love.

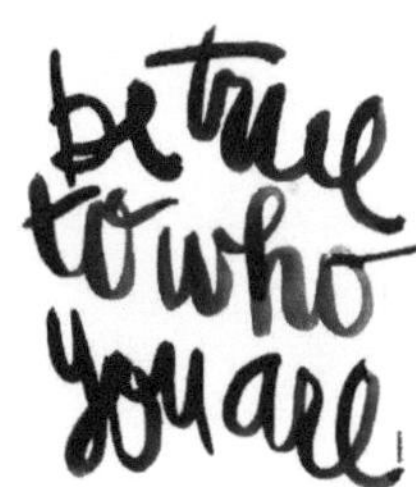

Rite and sorrow

I am the rite and the sorrow.
I am the heart and the gasping.

Here is the how
Here is the why.
Here is the turn of this dire wheel.

Keep faith, keep true.
Unearth the straight need.

I am the heart and the sorrow,
inelegant indecency.

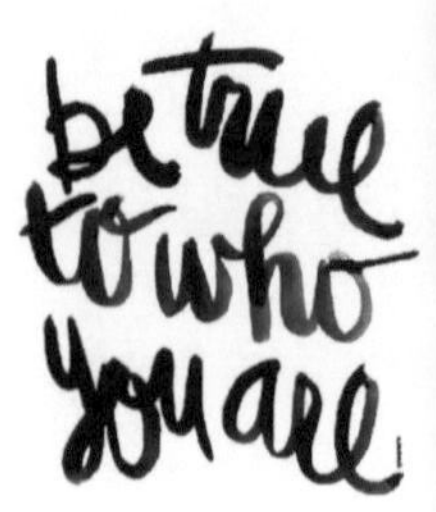

All that we have

Solemn we shall envy the quietness of nights.
Slowly we shall reveal what's the hurt, what's the joy.

We shall hear the lament of worn generations.

    Shall we thus just recant?
    Should we thus just regret?
    Should we even renounce?

We have just that one fear, that our world turns blind.

But,
    We do not know of fright.
We have climbed.
    We have resisted.

We have sung in the face of rightful anger.
We have given our souls to laziness and sin,
unforgiven even by the meaning of self.

We shall, shall we not, enter the cleft wondrous?
Solemn, shall we hurt?

Struggling

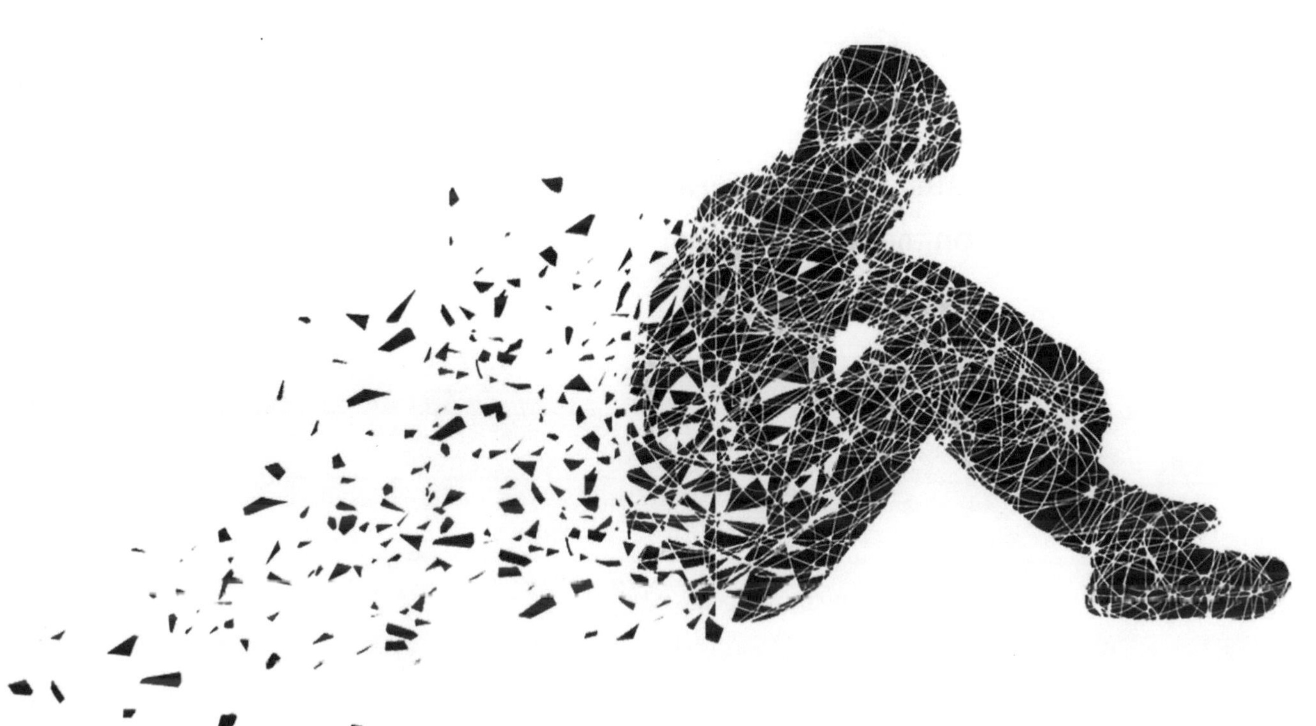

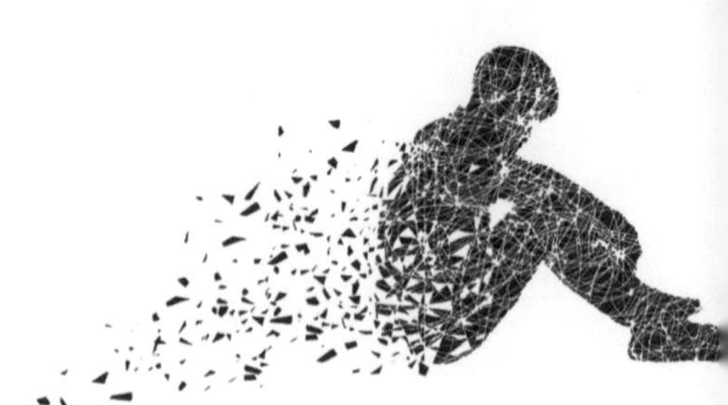

Return to War

When the soldiers went to the wars,
Anguish engraved in their deep sunken eyes,
There were brutal shooting stars
Striking over the sky of their rage.

Their arrogance was high, their despair tangible.
Their yearning created from the dust and the spit.

Created in anguish as a vise on their limbs,
as on the horizon wither those phantom clouds.

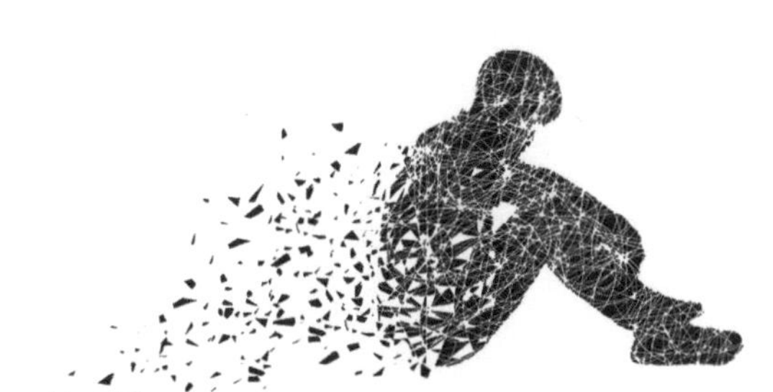

Danger time (an astonished song)

It was a time of rage
It was a time of danger.
Days on the raft of time.
Nights of desperate anger.
Wants torn asunder.
Needs in the winds of time.

It was a time of danger
and infinite frenzy.
It was a time of burning hearts
and a time of raising light.

Where were you, angry people?
Where were you, people of fright?
Who were you, people of anger?
Who were you, people of light?

It was a time of danger
and a time of great sweetness.
The waters tasted bitter
and the sunlight was feeling wrong.

These were the times of magic
of warriors and creators.
Those were the times of rising
of rebellion and of sweet hope.

Days of astounding noise.
Days of atonement.
Sins non committed.
Regrets without blessing.
Days of astounding light.
Days of kindness and fright.

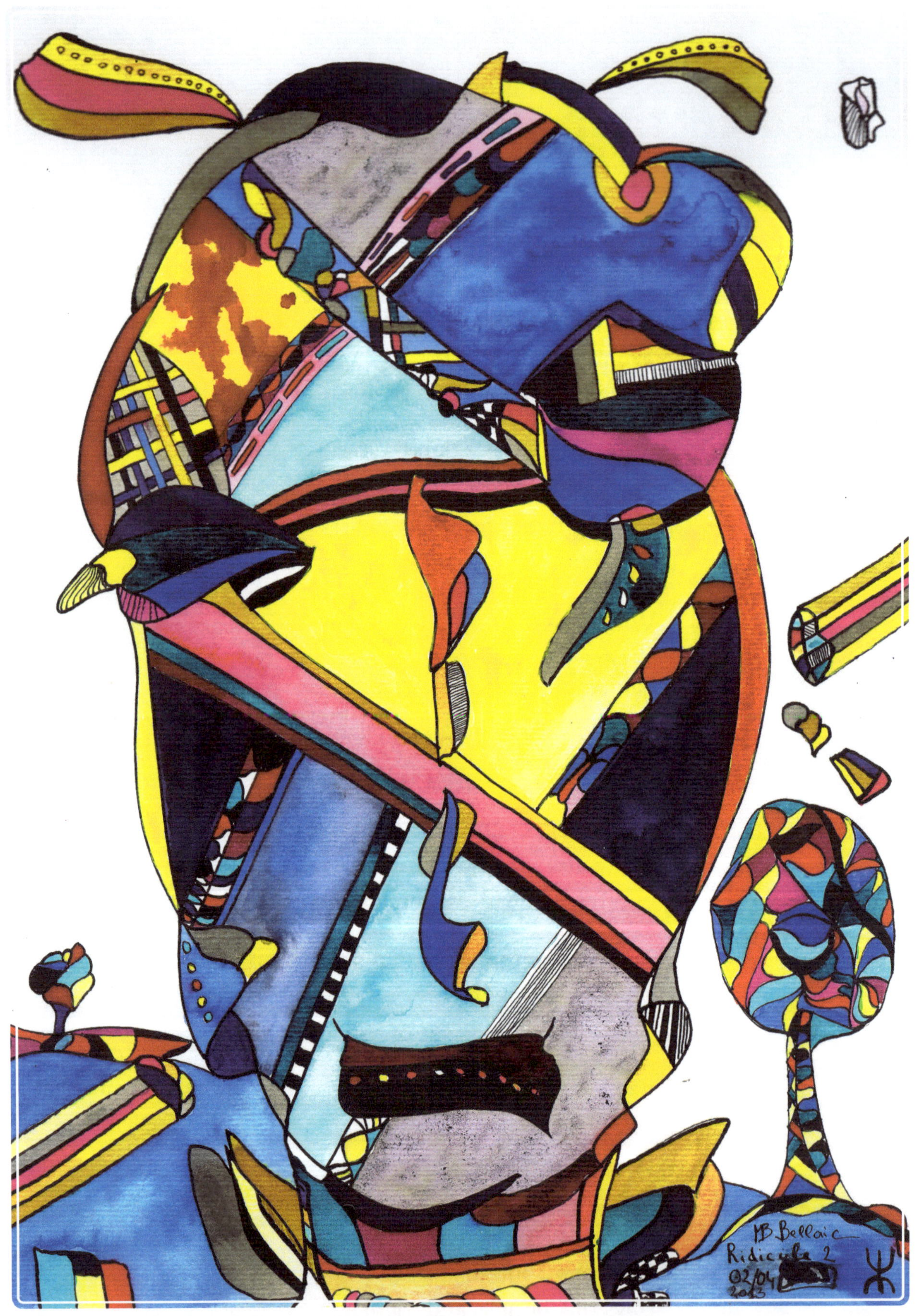

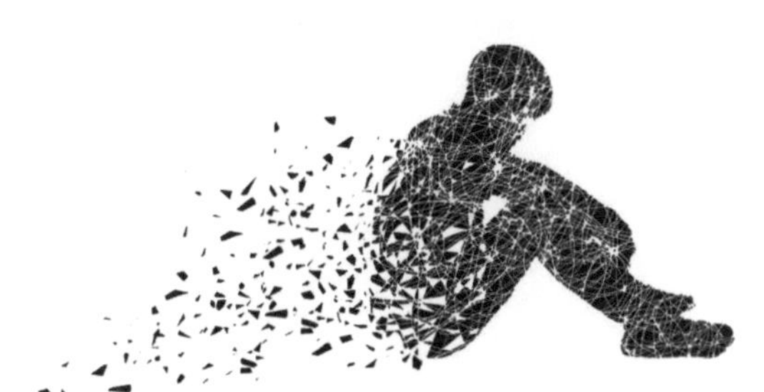

Balkan ballad

There is no shade in the shadows.
There is no harm in questioning.
The long river is running low
across the plains of mindlessness.

There is no shade in the shadows.
Death is remote; fear is absent.
The suffering is far below.

Roll on an on these long waters.
Here are the roads that lead nowhere.
There's a village on that sad plain
where nobody ever wonders.

Nothing's moving.
Nothing's right.
What did happen to all the years?

There is no shade in the shadows.
There are no doors towards our dreams.
None is winning; none is crying.
Where did they go, all our despairs?

Murky river,
capricious skies.
The long river is running low
unto this plain built of shadows.

There is no harm in the shadows.
Shades of our souls will get their rest.

.... Balkan ballad (cont.)

We found our flesh in the shadows,
we trusted,
we loved,
we were betrayed.
Shards of our souls have found their rest.

The long river is running dry
Killing all hopes of redemption.

There is a plain in the shadows.

Self-portrait with blues

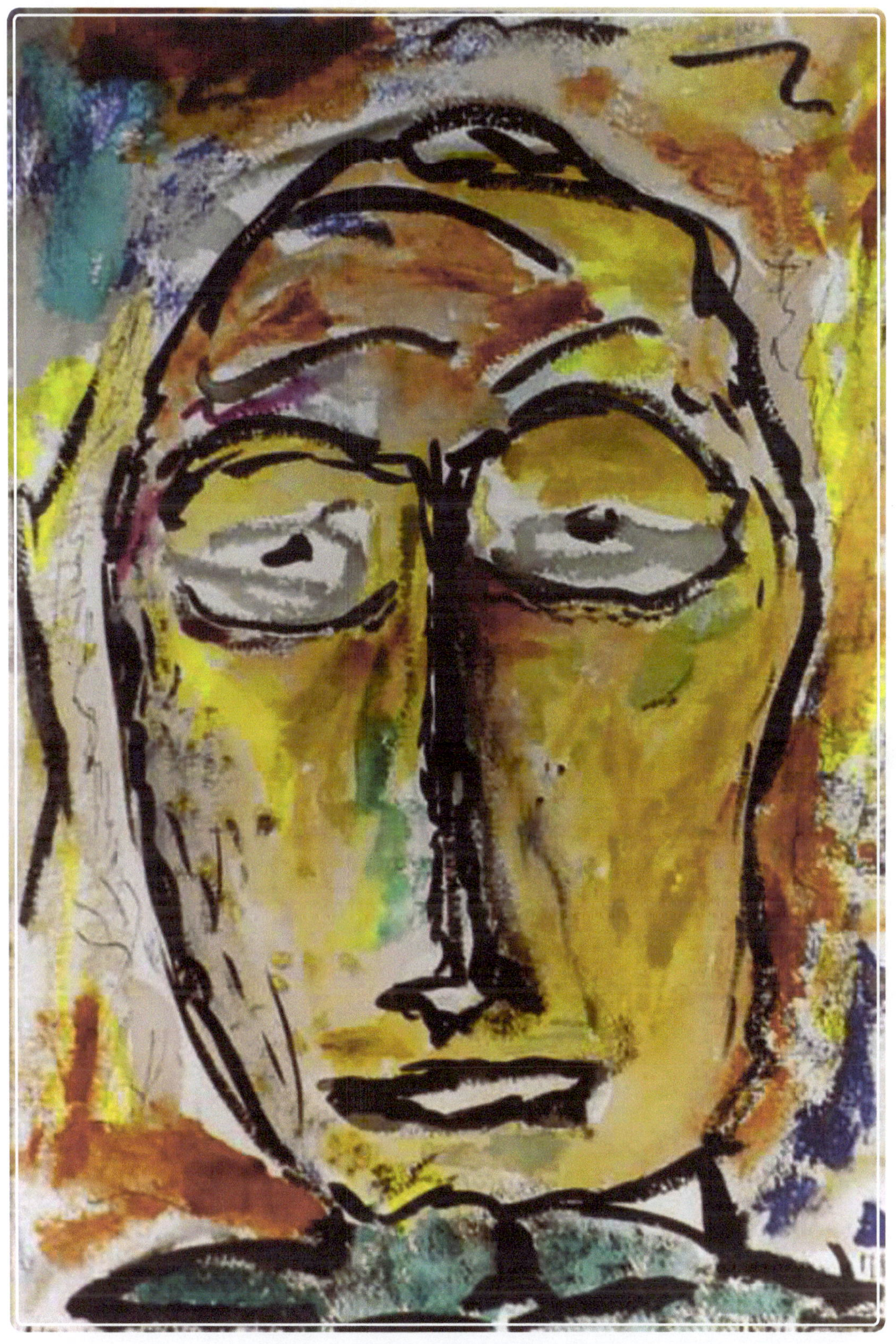

Poetry for....
That's all for now